FOR YOUR SAFETY PLEASE HOLD ON

For Your Safety Please Hold On

Kayla Czaga

NIGHTWOOD EDITIONS

2014

Third printing, 2018

Nightwood Editions
P.O. Box 1779
Gibsons, BC V0N 1V0
Canada
www.nightwoodeditions.com

TYPOGRAPHY & COVER DESIGN: Carleton Wilson
COVER IMAGE: Bird and tulip recreated based on Hungarian Folk Art.

Canada

Canada Council for the Arts
Conseil des Arts du Canada

Nightwood Editions acknowledges financial support from the Government of Canada and the Canada Council for the Arts, and from the Province of British Columbia through the British Columbia Arts Council and the Book Publisher's Tax Credit.

This book has been produced on 100% post-consumer recycled, ancient-forest-free paper, processed chlorine-free and printed with vegetable-based dyes.

Printed and bound in Canada.

LIBRARY AND ARCHIVES CANADA CATALOGUING IN PUBLICATION

Czaga, Kayla, author
For your safety please hold on / Kayla Czaga.

Poems.
ISBN 978-0-88971-303-1 (pbk.)

I. Title.

PS8605.Z34F67 2014 C811'.6 C2014-905169-7

for my parents

CONTENTS

I

Mother & Father

FUNNY

On the bus today, a man looked like you with your teeth
removed, his lips a wild party on his face. Father, you
are not yet dead, though doctors keep removing bits
of you. *Soon you'll carry me around, a few floaters in a jar,*
you shout through the phone. That shouldn't be funny,
but is, the way it was funny you telling me to apologize
to objects I bruised myself on as a child—*Don't tell me
you hurt the cupboard door.* It stopped me from crying.
In this city where so many beggars look like you, I am
stitching what I know about you into poems, sewing you
together before you die, before I have to oblige you
by just dumping your body into the ocean. How do I say
you loved my mother through thirty years of sickness
alongside your love of pork 'n' beans and Pilsner? To what
do I affix your Russian moustache? I know I will never fit
in the fishing lessons I failed, the grey days I wandered
away from you into the bushes. Father, I never told you—
I drank river water; I flipped over dead fish with a stick.

BIOGRAPHY OF MY FATHER

Mother's kidneys fail us.

After they airlift her to Prince George, he asks
me to pack sandwiches and silence.
We follow her in his black pickup. We leave
lights on in the living room.

A surgeon once lost a small mirror inside my father.

Gas station apples, black coffee.
Every other traveller is tired and suspicious.
My father is a casual nudist.

He spent 1970 in Stanley Park, without teeth.
It looked like this rest stop, south of Topley, where crows
fling their caws at passing motorhomes. Paperless outhouses,
but he's used to that. He tattooed his initials
into his own forearm.

Centreline like a migraine, all morning.
Paper cups of coffee. Radio stations
through towns—songs about love,
about killing men for less.

He bought my mother two taxidermied owls.
He bought a set of teeth because he wanted to marry her.

A butterfly pinned under the wipers. A moose
on the shoulder. Seventeen out-of-province licence plates
since Kitimat. My father takes nothing lightly. He didn't speak
until I was ten. His skin drags him low, toward earth.

Another small town, coffee refill
in some local joint with a waitress named Ruth.
My father invented alligators. His country
discovered sorrow.

Before I was born, he pawned
his shadow. He has no more
to sell for my mother.

The pines are purpled with pine beetle.
A porcupine is upturned by a red truck.
The sky above Burns Lake looks broken
into. Rain batters the water.

It's late. My father's hands failed at holding up
the day. The sun set regardless of his efforts.
He rents a room for me, but sleeps beside
the Skeena in the back of his truck. As a child,
he learned English from an Eaton's catalogue—
sleeping bags and fishing tackle—he speaks
to keep the world in place.

Morning comes on like the flu,
unapologetic—I hate the way
daylight tastes on a road trip.

Feet on the dash. Asleep on the dash.

I have a memory of my father in which he shaved
his beard.

I have a memory of my father holding a rubber chicken.

The night I was born, he won a bowling tournament.

I have a memory of my father—

he has vaccine scars on both shoulders,
aluminum burns down both arms.

Before the paramedics took my mother away,
my father kissed her little earlobes.

Past Vanderhoof, he drives
like a man with a mouthful of blood.
His glasses are comically large.
His hair is white and he loves her
silently through construction zones,
down Highway 16.

OBSERVATIONS

The television flickered, interviewed
itself. It glared across my father's glasses. His eyes
were sports updates. Salt on the coffee table, salt
in his soda, potato chips. Three sleeping pills at night.

His cat curled into ashes, in an urn on the fireplace.
It's hard to believe he snuck into Canada for this
life, this floral couch in a house too big
for three people. I spent my adolescence asking

about Hungary, on a bench in our front yard,
while the neighbour lady suntanned on her tarmac
driveway. Every conversation we've had could fit
in his ashtray. Instead of his life, my father

spoke of fiscal reports, the NDP, wars
in other parts of the world—*current affairs,*
he called them. In a language I didn't know,
my father spoke only mouthfuls of smoke.

MY FATHER, WINNING ME $242 AT THE KITIMAT GOLF & COUNTRY CLUB, LAST CHRISTMAS

Order anything you like. Tell them
it's for John. That's George Chow, general manager
of the hospital. See that tell? He's got pocket kings.

Dealer's Danny—real bigwig, head honcho of something
or other. Your mother doesn't like him much. *Call.*
Call. Club soda, ice, no straw. That's Pooga. Serious.

His real name. And that's Ken, Gus's son. We play
Gus's memorial tournament every May. Ken's
probably the only one at this table who hasn't played

his dad. Some nights I get here first and watch the golfers
down below. Did I ever tell you about my first job
rounding up golf balls from the lake—this was in Lethbridge.

I sold 'em back to the golfers. *All in*—I'm just playing
for fun tonight 'cause you're in town. S'alright, I've lost
my shirt dozens of times, hundreds. The first time

coming to Canada, fleeing Hungary. It was 1956,
the revolution. We travelled at night. Some Russians
shouted, *Come out, we won't shoot.* So my uncle

said, *John, give me your hand*—and I gave him my hand—
They won't shoot at kids. Then they started shooting.
Though I was only five, I remember the bullets touching

my hair, uncle folding behind me. Then your grandma
pulled me back into the bushes and we ran—my uncle's
blood on my back, no change of shirt 'til Canada.

HOCKEY

My father and I spent seventeen years in the basement
on brown floral couches watching the sucker
punch, the goalie fights, elbows to the face, pucks
lobbed over the glass and ricocheting off screen.
Those poor chumps in the penalty box watched
with us, their team getting walloped on the power play.
During commercial breaks, he explained *power play,*
icing and *offside.* It's been nearly a decade since
I've moved out and he still insists on phoning
during period breaks. He mutters insane love
for the goalie of the Calgary Flames, bets pennies
with relatives, receives ten-dollar bills wrapped
in newsprint in the mail. I still don't get hockey
or men who love hockey; men who miss their teeth;
the multitudes of men through frozen air whipping
white towels. What if, I ask, the Zamboni broke
down, would the fans spill out of the arena's belly,
a little drunk and nationalistic, ready to smash
shopfronts over a bad call? Has a broken-English
locker-room interview ever been so incomprehensible
even the player misunderstood his answers? *No*
more questions, he says. *Game's back on.* Hockey
will be the last thing I understand about my father.
On the farm, he once told me, they would sit in
Grandpa's truck—forty below in northern Alberta—
listening to the game on the radio, the whole family
in knitwear, hunching in to hear it through the static.

FATHER UNREPAIRED

You won't tell me anything when I call
but I've heard that your hip flops
loose in its socket, that you now walk
like a grounded fish. Mother told me.
Finally, she can keep up. *Not bad,*
you answered, that time I asked
how you were, after you drove
for two days to a town north of Edmonton
to find out your mother had already died.
She had asked for you, repeated
a Hungarian word your younger brothers
were too dumb or drunk to remember.
You came back with her blue gypsy lamp
in the passenger's seat, your hands
permanently curved to the wheel.
After that, you quit smoking
inside the house. You shattered your elbow
on the shed, lost a fingernail at work.
Last winter, you called to tell me
about the unseasonable number
of robins—the weather in your hip
that day, the storm a few miles off
and the robins—how their burnt song broke
your sleep before another twelve-hour
shift at the aluminum plant.
Check the weather, you said.
I bet we're in for it.

ANOTHER POEM ABOUT MY FATHER

I don't *get* poetry either. Mostly I get cavities,
junk mail. Once, I got eleven hundred dollars
in small change from my father for Christmas.
He said, *You've got to work for your money*—
meaning you've got to haul it through six feet
of snow to the bank, *Good luck, here's a bag.*
My father is more like a poem than most poems
are. He once tucked a living loon into his coat
and brought it home to amuse my mother who
loves birds, especially surprised-sounding birds,
especially owls. My nostalgia receptors zigzag
wildly through me when I think of my father
pushing his metal detector across all the parks,
schoolyards and riverbanks of this great nation,
waving it back and forth—*like some sort of*
yayhoo, my mother would say—until it beeps
solemnly above a nickel. With a butter knife
he cuts such slender metaphors from the earth.

WILD LILAC

That time from a provincial park I stole
wild lilac with my mother and gardened it
into the backyard. Those times into her arms
made of fabric softener I ran, my skirt
flapping in the breeze. The time we drove
for sandwiches together to the next town
over with the radio and windows open.
The time she bought me a fairy journal
in Great Falls, Montana. The private time
we fled to the movies to escape family
reunion time. All that time before the time
she started dying, how there was less
of it and somehow more than enough.
Now there's not enough and too much
sitting in doctors' offices with expired
magazines. How hard it is to move through.
How over it my mother is crumbling.
Time's a drag and with it drags the light,
the lilac blossoms into lilac dust. But how
lovely the lilac vanishing in the low dusk,
the petals deadlining all over the lawn.

WILDEST DREAMS

This morning above my apartment, a plane
pulled the slogan, REACH YOUR FULL POTENTIAL,
FIND OUT HOW TODAY, followed by
an unreadable-in-the-wind web address.
From my bed, I watched it drift, dipping
south. Every night, my mother straps
into her apnea suit, orbiting the ever-distant
planet of sleep. Dear Daniel Scott,
who in the third grade prayed,
Lord, I want to be a fire truck,
I'm sorry your dreams have by now
burnt out. Dear Travis Zentner of Cornerstone
Funeral Home, did you at six know
you wanted to peddle coffins and dip
our dead in embalming fluid, or did you wish
to win the Stanley Cup, annually
skating backwards through thirty
North American cities? And what
did my mother dream before her dreams
started skipping like old CDs? *I quit,*
she says, *breathing seventeen times*
an hour. At sixty-two years old,
she's a sleep astronaut. Her CPAP presses
positively on her airways, waits on her
bedside table through waking hours.
In airports, the escalators go
despondent when people aren't on them,
slow. If only we had been designed
with as much focus. I wanted to help
animals and then someone explained

"put down" to me. I wanted a horse
as big as my imagined Nebraska,
cantering. Adults kept asking what
I wanted to be, and now I'm the adult
asking inward. I still don't know.
For a while after the machine arrived,
my mother woke each day
believing each day would be better
than the previous. Then the daily routine
painted the same-old beige over them.
For a while my full potential flapped
around overhead before crash
landing into the fairgrounds.

SONG

Outside my window, seagulls and crows continue
the discourse on language, insisting it need not be beautiful
to be song. If song accompanies their shallow black
and white bickering over garbage at 5 A.M., do I still believe

language needs to be beautiful? Their insistent discourse
pecks holes in the morning. Here I am still trying
to believe, at 5 A.M., despite the bickering over garbage
because faith describes perfectly how my mother is dying.

Here I am still trying to peck holes in the morning;
song is just another word I use for wanting
faith to describe how perfectly my mother is dying
thousands of miles away, in a small town I rarely visit.

Song is just another word I want to use.
Illness is just another word. Mother is just a word
thousands of miles away, in a small town I rarely visit.
The winter light pours slowly into my window.

Illness is just a word. Mother is just a word
with someone in it. Can I sing without words?
The slow winter light pours through my window.
Long after I've stopped making sense, I'm just a sound

with someone in it. Can I sing without words
and still be song, accompanying the crows, shallow and black,
making sense with just sounds? Long after I've stopped,
seagulls and crows continue outside my window.

II

The Family

THE FAMILY

The religious aunt lolls in a lawn chair, large and alone.
Her moustache twitches, as she dreams of the Lord's
clean feet. Summer's end barbecue. The family
unwraps hot dogs. How is your brother doing? Long
eye-contact, porch lights yellowing into autumn.
The family passes around a comatose kid, his lips
edged Doritos-orange. Who does this one belong to?
Eat something. The family smells of barbecued
corn, dry leaves, cheap beer. The family smells
of family to discourage touching. The family is/n't
speaking and (dis)approves of your engagement.
Eat more. The family has bad tans, forgiving slacks
and mushroom noses. Go thank Grandma Marie.
A young cousin, is she fifteen already, spreads her body
into a cornfield and whispers stories to her sister
of an estranged uncle, her third-generation curiosity.
Staring off down the gopher hole, the family will
(not) reconcile, slouching in lawn chairs until dawn.
A matter of money. Eat more. Aunty Dorothy
(by marriage) scoops third servings of potato salad
onto soggy paper plates, better finish it off. Better sit
with the drunk uncles. When you were yay-big
the family changed your diapers. Of all the unruly
English teeth. When you were ten, the family got you
drunk at a cousin's wedding and you walked naked
for miles until the family found you, lifted you
into its large cotton shirt and carried you home.

THE GRANDFATHER

His wife predeceased him, his parents
and seven siblings. His microwave.
The orange bush that bloomed
in the rafters of his carport went
a winter too soon. The VHS
was born and died in his lifetime.
Every border of Europe lifted
and shifted. All around the world
people predeceased him at a rate
of 1.78 people per second.
He sat in his burgundy recliner
watching the wind froth clouds,
the trees keeling, bowing
to the long horizon, gradually
predeceasing himself.

THE GRANDMOTHER

Snapdragons, wild garlic, her loose arms
hugging closed her cardigans, touring
you around her garden. You visited her
for two weeks each summer. How strange
you must've seemed, taller every time,
a girl perhaps she hardly recognized
except for her daughter's eyes planted
into your face. Still, she hugged you
in the carport, scooped pistachio
ice cream while the family rearranged
vehicles and luggage. You liked her tiny
silver spoon collection hung beside
the comically large ceramic spoon
and fork knick-knacking her kitchen
wall. You remember the time she swore
at the laundry machine for breaking;
the way she asked everyone how
many potatoes they wanted for dinner
and cooked exactly that number.
A silly old child she seemed, so small
in fuchsia lipstick and lilac slacks
billowing out from her twig body.
When she died you had just started
university in a new city and weren't
allowed to attend her funeral. Your
mother says you look like her, but can't
explain how—same face, she says,
except the features. She shows you
a far-off photo, sepia-toned, a girl
overexposed, squinting into the sun.

THE OTHER GRANDMOTHER

Your other grandmother told you the bunnies
were in the freezer. She was a hoot, owling outside
the barn. She swept up chickens and spooked
horses with her sure, short saunter.

Your other grandmother walked barefoot
across Europe with your infant father. She spun
the yarn, yanked the chain, hogwashed floors
until her face shone blue in them.

Your other grandmother dredged dinner, floured
her sons' fish tales, fried every word in butter.
A crystal bowl of chokecherries for dessert.

Your other grandmother drank her husbands
under the coffee table. She slapped your cheeks
with stories, kissed you with myth, carried
on into all hours, carrying children on
both her hips and shoulders.

Your mother always dreaded the arrival
of your other grandmother who brought
the not-grandfathers with her. The RV
of them smoking and drinking in the driveway.

Your other grandmother smuggled firearms
across the border, drove without
mirrors, the family wicked with worry.

She taught you all about cancer. You loved
her blue bald head, the way she curled
beside you in bed, warming your cold
feet between her calves, while snoring.

THE NOT-GRANDFATHERS

The not-grandfathers were not
your grandfathers. They were also not

not your grandfathers. They bought
you beaded moccasins, filled your pockets

with watermelon hard candies. The not-grandfathers
appear variously in photographs with the other

grandmother, looking like men
who loiter in Tim Hortons

on Saturday mornings. They wore cardboard
trousers, pen protectors in breast pockets, liver

spots on forearms. The not-grandfathers
were rented from other families, rewound

and returned. One summer, two not-grandfathers
fought in your driveway. Another asked you to call him

Lionel. Those marshals of confusion
commanded pickup trucks

and temporary carrots in the garden. Old
orphans dangling outside

of the family on every greeting card
occasion, not sure

whether or not to touch you.
Eventually, they carried you on their shoulders

so you could see the parade. You stared down
into their not-familiar hairlines,

the grey folds behind their ears,
and wondered who they really belonged to.

THE DRUNK UNCLE

Funny bone of every family. Wears
the same old skull T-shirts for thirty years
to unnerve his mother. Grunts his monosyllabic
moniker—*Bob, Tom or Lou*—at whomever
he's introduced to. *Go ahead,* he winks. Pull
his finger. Braid his chest hair. Top of the odd-
job totem pole. King of the all-you-can-eat.
Aficionado of the naked lady tattoo. Won third
in a moustache competition, punched out first
place. Too young to have fought in Nam,
but knows a guy who knows a guy with no
thumbs. Did time a bunch of times—asks, *You
need meth, machine guns, snake's blood?*

Late to your wedding in an alligator tuxedo,
he staggers straight into the open bar. Resurfaces
for his too-loud lecture on the hullabaloo
of marriage. And he'd know from his three*, all
great ladies, mind you.* He bends the conversation
to confess he's a lesbian. Wrestles his nephews
one-armed and wins, tosses squealing nieces.
Chases them around the buffet brandishing
dentures. Roughhouse inventor. Unexpected
best friend of the religious aunt, he pecks her
cheek as they hobble the two-step. Begins

his stories, *I has a buddy up in Fort St. James, summering in Timbuktu.* Has buddies for every
occasion. You can tell it'll be long yarn,
the way his eyes roll up into the water spot
on the ceiling above your head. He yammers
the nails, beats the dead horse, bags the wind,
blows it hot and beery into your face.
It's a slow shit, man, he whistles, staring
cockeyed into the world's faulty wiring.

THE DECORATIVE AUNT

She had you by the elbow at PLEASE
SEAT YOURSELF. Now you're staring with her
into her phone at photos of her dog
in costume: as a doctor, a hot dog,
some famous person's daughter's dog.
Your sweet 'n' sour pork congeals
as she speaks, a gelatinous mass.
In the orange gleam of heating lamps
her face looks like a military cot
you could bounce a quarter off.
Already twentysomething with no
husband in sight, she winks.
Immediately you want to recircle
the buffet like a stuffed vulture, slop
another carbohydrate on your plate.
Resist the urge to add to your padding,
dear. She resisted and hooked her dentist,
winks, *the doctor and missus*—
everyone she knows knows how
much she likes how that sounds. She
of the Ativan-eyed side of the family,
bejewelled and bleached, leather-shoed
from therapeutic tanning bed snoozes.
Her Canadian tuxedo tailored tight
the way Dr. Uncle Toni likes it.
You could waste all day, here, in this
Albertan Chinese dive featuring
a sorry tank of tilapia and flat screens
on every surface. They go dead or off
if you look away for too long.

THE RELIGIOUS AUNT

Her basic cable-knit is full of reruns—
Wheel of Fortune loops over and over
holes in the program. Photo albums fat
with duplicates: Abigail doggy-paddling
in a fuchsia two-piece beside Donovan
knee-deep in gunk, April '92. A mauve
yawn slung over the old sofa. Her ears
are pansies dried in a Bible. A string
of dollar-store pearls buttresses her
bifocular eyes. Her breath is the place
a younger her sat down in and died.
She lopes to the kitchen to shake out
a snitch from her tin of tarts. Her water
cooler murmurs Proverbs to the wall
while her cross-stitch awkwardly petitions
God—*God bless, God keep, God rest*—
she's waited sixty-three years for a response
from that upstairs shmuck while the world's
kicked up such colourful ruckus, such
a vibrant hubbub. She's the slow centre
of a central vac, dizzy just watching it
technicolour its wayward way, sucking
up dust, day after day after day.

III

For Play

FOR PLAY

1.
This is a game for girls: putting a hat
on the cat, putting pants on
the cat, drawing a turkey by tracing
her hand. Little girls like cats.

2.
A dress is a game with armholes.
A dress is played with a waistband.
A waistband is a game with a firm
winner and sore loser. A dress is
plaid or floral or polkas. Dispersed
vertically with gathers, a dress is
a selection of flowers in a dancehall.
A waistband plays flat music a little
girl will twist. This is a set list. You
play a girl by flipping through her.

3.
the girl crayons *little girls are like that*
the little boy is blue
the duck is yellow
the duck is yellow tumbles forever into the green lake
the beginning of the black cat waxes in the red tree
the little girl is a sweet sad colour—bruised or blushing?
the little girl holds out her blank hands toward the little boy is blue
the little girl holds out her hands filled with *little girls are like that*
the sweet sad colour accumulates in the pencil sharpener

the little girl tumbles forever into the boy is blue
the little boy is blue accepts *little girls are like that*
the little girl is faceless until she colours it on

4.
A girl is game with how many licks
gets to her centre. Little girls like
a firm licking. Little girls play will he
call on the third or fourth day
after a successful date. Little girls
play Friday flip-up day. What did
he mean, keep it casual? What did
he mean, that girl is asking for it?
A girl replays twenty unsayable
questions in her head. Little girls
lose the game inside their heads.
What was she asking for, exactly?

GERTRUDE STEIN LOVES A GIRL

one—a girl

When she walks on the hopscotch, o yes,
a girl lights up. A girl is a gain, again
and she jumps, o yes, lights up. A girl is
a lips, a blip topped with blonde frizz,
jumping. A twaddle in chips. A bright
bit of a trip. A girl in stirrups is a sugar,
a spice and everything burning nice.
A girl's burning earlobes, when she hears
me, o yes, she is a bounce and a going.

two—a two of girls

A girl will sometimes pair, hold hands, skip
and be a horse, play house. A girl will share.
A girl will love another little girl if she is
Amanda and little and brown and lucky. A two
of girls is as cruel as exclusive. A two of girls
wrestles and throws each other from windows.
A two of girls plays Nintendo together and plays
Nintendo together and plays Nintendo together.
A two is two different girls, girls, girls. A two
of girls yells at their mothers for each other.
A two of girls sleeps over and over. A two
of girls stomps and cries and hates her and
phones her afterwards for a come over later.

three—never woman

A girl never wants to woman. A girl is kicked
and killed in wild, howling womanhood.
Jealousy is lousy and beginning to look
womanish, moustached. Jealousy is without
tricks. Nail polish picked at, recklessly chipped.
Girls win and are not jealous. Girls never exhibit
green edges. Girls are not greedy but always
given in to. A toonie for her Saturday wants
and frills and flounces. O yes and thank you!
Jealousy is the stick of an ugly girl, a surly girl
with hairy forearms. A girl turns another girl
womanish to stay small and wanted and win.

four—a girl by her mother

In picked outfits, she is crossed legs
and lilies. She is mine and mimes swell.
A girl is given dolls to mirror or she is
a far fat turkey. She does so for she is a
fine yes, fair Sunday. She is a frequent
purge, toilet bowler. So slim and isn't it
just so. Isn't it just so. A little bit with limbs
she is, she's slim and isn't it just so.
She wipes her lips on damp dish cloths.
She sits. She sips her bright pink fingers.
She slips into smart short haircuts, yes,
she does so, and does herself up just so.

five—girls and men and want

How many sweet sinisters turn into spinsters
over men; how many men are into little girls
blessed with elbows and belly buttons; how
many lips are puckered into blood blisters;
how men hold their shoulders slowly, hold
little girls' slow shoulders; how little girls like
strawberry yogurt and men; how little girls
want wrong men, men with audible problems,
men with holes, men without homes or usable
pockets; how with welted red want; how
little girls want and want to fix them.

A FEW BOYS, JULY 1997

a few boys set fire to their shorts, a few threw sticks for big black dogs, one rode his wheelchair to the Kit-Kat store, a few disturbed shit, a few had it coming, some jerks and some nice young boys, a few flirted, one helped his girl into a tree, a few caught fire, jumped over sprinklers, a few rode scooters, fewer drove cars, a few listened to rude music at the gym and were asked to turn it down but they didn't, so a few were followed and shot down by the creek—three killed, a few photos on the evening news even though it was only a small-town crime, only a few boys—a few were just a shame, a few still pedalled blue bicycles, a few stopped at the half-mast flag and felt ashamed, and went on collecting frogs

SOME GIRLS, JULY 1997

some girls were sad, some girls were worried, some girls were Amanda, some girls were Kerrie and Erica, some girls jumped off swings, some girls swung higher, some girls wore stirrup pants, some girls ran naked, some girls were the sum of their parts, some freckled shoulders and just-before boobs, some girls weren't, some girls ate only orange Skittles, some girls murdered Barbies and some Barbies deserved it, some girls held hands, some girls held some girls under porches and forced kisses, some uncomfortable touching some girls, some girls were pinched, some girls were bitten and kicked, some girls couldn't tell their mothers where those bruises came from, some girls just couldn't remember, some girls were afraid of closet alligators, some were afraid their windows would open, some girls were worried, some girls were sad

LITTLE VILLAIN

Mother said, *Sickness*
is the first indication of children, and the clouds

peeled back like scabs. Bright enough
to magnify ants, August hung in sticky
strips. Air orangish, sidewalk-scented.

I put caterpillars in pickle jars and poked
no holes. I drank fruit punch
to excess. Inside, mother reclined

on the floral couch, books alphabetically
beside her. She swallowed vitamins
with ice cubes and said, *When your friends visit,*

slingshots are forbidden. So, I constructed
a catapult from Popsicle sticks and loved
the boy who twisted

until birds broke, filled his pockets
with small bodies, filled my body
with bruises, a pleasant swelling. His name

was William. A jump rope looped around
his dog's neck, pulled taut 'til the dog
coughed and the rope bloodied, and blood

puddled on the back porch under Mother
when she saw us, a small scream
falling from her. Sirens sliced the air

into little Jell-Os and a set of gloved hands
placed her back on the couch where she stayed.
After me, she had problems conceiving.

She named him John. After him,
she stopped completely.

WILLIAM COOK

Summer break and he's sticky
with it—buzz cut and Popsicle-lipped, barefoot
and stepping on bees, hollering

You 'n' whose army? at anyone, bullying cats
and the kids next door, the kids down the street,
the kids in the wading pool filled

with pee and laughs, *Slap ya into next*
week, fruit loops. Got bicycle, will pedal.
Got slingshot and one arm

in a sling, but you should see the other
kid. *Go sign his cast, will ya?* The brute
going into grade two, William Cook.

His daddy's in the navy and mom's skirts
shortening with another brother. But Bill
will always be the biggest, the most jeans

ripped. Always the shit disturber from way
back. But you should've seen him
that day in July; it would've broke

your heart—that grass-stained darling
almost looked sorry. The semi-circle
of kids gawking, *Did he do it?*

The limp-sock with wings—*Bet he did*—
slip-necked robin in his hand, light
as a hot dog. *Ma, don't be*

so mad, said the boy with ears too-big
gone red trying to rebuild the bird.

EYE EXAM

do you see the big *E* is that better do you see the big *E* this side or this side follow my finger here or here this side or this side

identify the little girl among the other figures *a* or *b*

who is she next to or is she isolated read the story is that a *c* pinch the fly's wings here or here read the story when will the edges turn orange here or here when will the edges turn orange

or is she isolated pinch the fly's wings trace the number nine look at my ear

identify her feelings look at my ear read the story reread the story

count her stuttering fingers

or is she isolated

does she puddle at the lash line or are the lights sloppy

is she happy or sad

or are her boots fuchsia

can you see her stuttering fingers here or here trace the number nine is that a *c*

do the black spots belong to her

does the weather change her irrevocably

does her coat match her hat

does she dissolve look at my ear here or here

MAD MINUTE

9	7	9	0	4	9
× 2	× 9	× 3	× 9	× 9	× 8

can she finish it in a minute
can she *four times six*
can she finish it
can she see that man through the window, legless from where the
wall hits
can she finish it in a minute
is the minute ticking
is the minute's red pressure ticking in her ears and the skin of her neck
is her mother weeping into her own lap
is the girl just a bit of her mother, sitting in the world as if she existed
is the world thirty questions split into columns and rows to be
finished
can she finish it
can she smell the hamster rotting on its wheel
can she see that man, moving leglessly about the playground
can she finish it with a birthday party pencil in her hand
is *six times six is thirty-six* in her mother's cloying voice inside her head
is it disappointment
is the man multiplying her mother's fears, moving leglessly beside the
play structure
is this the world, then, the legless man, the minute ticking, her mother
saying, *eight times seven is fifty-six, seven times seven is forty-nine, you know
this, you do, just finish it*

GONE IS THE VHS. GONE IS THE WHIR.

Gone are the days of dawdling
alphabetically through Blockbuster
pretending to be cool in proximity
to our parents, hot and awkward
in our jackets, hiding ratings under
our thumbs. Goodbye bargain bin
depots, you despots of popular
culture, Pez-dispensers of trend.
No more scrawny nerds in blue
smocks scoffing at our rom-coms. No
more overdue movies lost under
chesterfield cushions. No more NO
MORE LATE FEES, which were just
late fees with new pseudonyms.
I do not mourn, o Blockbuster,
your bankruptcy, though I loved
zooming downtown with my mom
seconds before 6 P.M. to drop tapes
through your slot, that three-metre
dash to your door. It's not you
but the feeling of a movie I miss—
that 7-oz. box with rattling innards.
Gone is the VHS. Gone is the whir
and click, rewinding the ribbons
on which our movies were printed.
Gone, like pogs and Pluto, are those
plastic black cassettes with windows
I imagined mini actors trapped
behind, fondly waving goodbye.

I FORGOT TO MENTION THE THUNDERBALL

The day I stepped through my Etch
A Sketch signalled the end of an era.
Over were the evenings my father
would lie belly-down on the rumpus
room rug, propped on his elbows
winding mini-mazes for me to solve,
as I counted bunnies on his Pilsner
bottle. All I remember about Nicky
Schrier is plastic pucks clicking
back and forth on her air hockey table
in the bruised glow of her mauve
glitter lamp. I remember the sound
of Polly Pocket dolls shuddering
up the vacuum cleaner. I remember
gel pens, pens with glowing ends,
glow-in-the-dark stars constellating
on all our bedroom ceilings below
which I'd temporarily scrawl *fuck*
on my Etch A Sketch until that day
my foot split its plastic screen.
Where in the landfill is my Styrofoam
solar system slowly leaking spray paint?
I'll never again live that morning
before the science fair, balancing
its coat-hanger frame on my lap
in the passenger seat of the Astrovan.
Like the mazes on my Etch A Sketch,
that day's long since been shaken
from the slate, nothing left of it,
but the memory gone blurry and grey.

IV

For Your Safety Please Hold On

23RD BIRTHDAY

In this city where all the shops stay open
the people close early. I closed. I told

another person, *I cannot*
love you anymore; please mail my books
back to me. Then I went bowling

and threw seven consecutive
balls into the gutter. Misery of the five-pin. I slept

in a bathtub. People keep buying me
clocks. Puddles keep collecting
sidewalks. Maybe I'll collect puddles

or clock out like so many people I've seen
on buses, that man who wept

violently into his scarf and the rest
of us trying to ignore him, turning up
our not-listening devices. Tonight

I am twenty-three and looking
for someone gentle enough to hold back

my hair—this could be you, stranger
with your three-point smile and hairdo.
Tonight I want to stop watching the clocks;

I fear I'll become them—spinning
in circles with hands covering my face.

VICTORIA SOTO

In the poem I show to no one, a young teacher hides
her students from a gunman, lifts
them into cupboards—her hands smoothing

their hair, closing cupboard doors. Thousands of miles
away, snow falls into a small northern town
where I write, *Twenty children fell as snow. The light*

turned less familiar as it reflected
off their bodies. I've never been to Connecticut,
but I imagine a town hall filled with photo albums,

yellow roses, teddy bears, family members circling small
tables, retelling the story of twenty
short lives—*They woke, ate cereal, and a stranger walked*

into their school with his hands full
of guns. I stay awake all night, clicking through holes
in the internet, finding her photo, Victoria, thumb-sized

with dark hair, light eyes, clear skin. She stared
directly into the camera and then, how much later, hid
children in cupboards and turned

to the shooter to collect a violence the television
calls "random." It turns over in me, repeats as snow
repeats—on the radio, television, in the thin voices

of my neighbours—*When twenty children fell,*
the world felt less familiar—and falling again with each
retelling, the snow and the stranger,

the teacher who smoothed their hair.

POETRY SHORTAGE

Rain again, blurring the world beyond the window.
Days slip off as I sit at my desk, vague
segments, named to give them shape—to say

on Monday I woke up and constructed a routine.
I ate through my life, sensing it was sufficient
if not memorable. *Time does not finish*

a poem—no, it finishes us. My houseplants shiver
with me into another winter of not thriving.
My cat's wet nose presses cold into my calf, tickles

like new snow. She curls into dark corners
to sleep. I think the world is running out
of poetry. We can't prove there will be more clear days

to compare to apples. Traffic shucks continually through
the rain, the din of it, muffling my head. The hum
that goes on with or without us, simply to go on. I hate

the things people tell me about art, creativity being this big
event we're all invited to. To me, it's always
been an ache I can't compare to anything

which I try to compare everything else to. I don't feel it
these days. The same old wind blows over buildings,
flapping like a mouth. I still wander, sometimes,

my coat closing the world out of my body, with pockets
full of garbage, with my slender, steady want. I still
make the bed and at bedtime unmake it.

MAY CONTAIN TRACES

In grade three I was jealous of the boy
who had an EpiPen, Aaron. With it,
he could survive peanuts. Like a video-game
egg it was hidden elsewhere to be uncovered
during moments of kingdom crisis.
In China, workers weave through fields
pulling paintbrushes across crops
for pollination, all the bees gone, fallen
onto sidewalks, a billion yellow blossoms
underfoot. Sadness crunches in me
as my mind's foot traipses over them,
over my misinformation of them.
I am not okay. I am spooning chemicals
into my mouth and calling them food.
My produce, hauled north for two weeks
from California, reeks of truck stop—
this apple could actually be a candle.
A classroom aid sprinted to Aaron
when he fell from his desk choking
on invisible intruders, his face swelling
purple. She crumpled him against her
chest, plunging the pen in. The classroom
held its collective breath. I wanted to be
held like that, protected from some
trace threat. I am still so misinformed
and selfish. See, I am tracing threats
onto my placemat, spelling them out
in 99¢ alphabet soup. Can someone please
tell me what's going on? My mouth feels
like it's hardened into plastic. I wish I

could live quietly in China, painting fruit
onto trees, thinking of the preservatives
sprinkled into me, thinking isn't it lovely
how someone wants to preserve me?

TEMPORARY

At the Ash Wednesday service, waiting
for the priest to cross my forehead, I watched him
touch the faces of the people in front of me,
mishearing him say, *Remember you are blessed.*
I was horrified when I remembered it
was really, *Remember you are dust,* with ashes
thumbed into my forehead. Headlights spattered
through the intentionally broken glass
windows of that beautiful downtown church
tucked behind a mall, as I tried to understand
and to dust you shall return. Traffic lights
flickered through Christ with arms nailed
open, Mary robed in blue, mourning into his feet.
After the service, I spilled out of the church
into wet February and public transit hauled me
back into my crumbling ordinary life. What
happens after this? When Jesus died,
it was temporary, the stone rolled away,
but where is he now, and can any of us hope
to go there, or is it all ashes to ashes and dust
covered bookshelves? Last week, Liz tried
to explain taxidermy to me, how she peeled
a rabbit, then rigged its pelt back into
rabbit-shape. She emptied a set of robin's wings
to sew onto its back—the flying rabbit.
It looked alive, a stitching trick, the way
my dead relatives look alive, resurrected
in photographs. It reminded me of colouring
Easter eggs with my mother. We blew the yolks
into a bowl before we dyed the shells

blue and yellow. How the eggs looked full
until we held them up to the light.

THAT GREAT BURGANDY-UPHOLSTERED BEACON OF DEPENDABILITY

Over dinner, my landlady laughs
about her day teaching rich Korean kids
the difference between a nightstand
and a one-night stand. Her son goes wild
for the bicycle pump. From his highchair,
he wails, erupting borscht. Refuses to sit
without its hard plastic denting his chin.
I don't get relationships. Once I got lace
panties in the mail from a friend who lives
in Winnipeg. He wrote, *I'm coming to visit*
you at Christmas! So I spent December
pretending to be busy, ice skating until
my feet purpled, wondering how love
could transpire so oppositely between two
people. My mother once loved a grey van so
completely she sat in it for twenty minutes
every winter morning while it defrosted.
They listened to the radio together, to her
favourite tapes. The van went everywhere
with her, unlike my father who plays poker.
It lived for thirteen years in our driveway,
a great burgundy-upholstered beacon
of dependability, until its engine went.
I want to climb into you and strap myself in,
but that's not really love. Instead, we idle
in separate uncertainties, exhausting
reassurances. You thank my landlady
for dinner and roll away into a night
that imperfectly intersects my own, and I try

to stop imagining the ways we could fail
each other, and the people in rooms
everywhere who are continually failing
each other, and hope toward someday
having one nightstand with you, maybe two.

POEM FOR JEFF

The Korean shopkeepers are fucked. The students reading
by the dim light of their textbooks are fucked. The couple
fucking on a kitchen table in a loft on Third Avenue is fucked.
The hipsters, plastered in wallpaper pants, blazing ambient
noises through hamburger headphones are fucked. Fucked
are the CEOs and the graceful lines of women buying oranges
in December. The senior citizens shivering in complexes.
The fucked mutter slender apologies to each other—I am sorry
your loved ones perished in a fire, that life has fucked you
with such regularity, there are no jobs or cities safely to live
in, I get it, Matthew Arnold's ignorant armies skirmish on,
making old the new year, again. The lady with bolts of hair
selling painted spoons down by the harbour is fucked blatantly
while others are fucked subtly, gradually over time, eroded
with great misguidedly fucked love and passivity, each howling
out a verse of the failing song of the fucked, and I know it
does not undo the fucking, but it's beautiful, sounding out over
the ocean, startling the exquisitely fucked heron into flight.

FOR YOUR SAFETY PLEASE HOLD ON

Another forty minutes in a stranger's armpit,
oh boy. How do you like avoiding eye contact
with me, sir in neon windbreaker?
Let's stare at the logos mass-embroidered
into each other's outerwear, listening
to whatever podcasts or pop music
the wires lift into our ears. So many
public strangers whose voices we never
hear. How do they sound murmuring
down the telephone's dark tunnel
toward loved ones? Staring at stickers
that in urgently red uppercase letters read,
FOR YOUR SAFETY PLEASE HOLD ON, I want to
graffiti, TO EACH OTHER, to the ends of them.
I'm sorry—love is ruining my sensibilities.
Above us, posters advertising education
and mortgage rates glow in blue light.
We contort to respect each other's personal
space, as the bus puts on passengers.
It's funny how distant you can remain
sharing oxygen and travel. It's funny how
your backpack says, *Honk if you like*
honking. Sir, I'm honking. For your safety
please hold onto each other, violently
on all the sofas, mattresses and futons
that fill your respective housing units.
Please hold on tightly to your beloveds,
who've miraculously not been flung
through the windshield while careening
through the city to return to you.

V

Many Metaphorical Birds

MANY METAPHORICAL BIRDS

> *Merely to say the same thing twice—language is language—how is that supposed to get us anywhere? But we do not wish to get anywhere. We would like only, for once, to get to just where we already are.*
>
> —Martin Heidegger

1

The Holy Spirit filled me
with that going-downhill-on-
rollerblades feeling.

Another day galloped
east faster than I could
say *Our Father*.

*

Lord, I once loved a boy
named Benjamin—you know
this—who taught himself

computer programming.
He spoke fluent Python,
muttered it to great effect

into his computer.
Calculators ran into being
on his screen. I loved him

like windshield wipers,
intermittently, eventually not
enough for either of us.

So now we are in different
time zones and I unpack
boxes filling up a new life.

*

The Lord told the Israelites, they
would be his people and he would be
their God. Thru the Book of Exodus

they followed and *Lord,* they
shouted, *weren't there graves*
enough for us in Egypt?

*

On Saturday at the café near
my new apartment, a barista
named Jeremy tried to explain

Heidegger's *Being and Time,*
as the café pumped floral
music into the air over and into

our heads, inducing *that café*
feeling. Jeremy said Heidegger
said transcendence is an activity.

Then he—Jeremy, though
probably also Heidegger—went
philosophically sweeping

the floors. What's the difference
between café and coffee
shop? On Sunday, Jeremy

wasn't there. Instead without
enthusiasm an older lady pulled
my espressos into a mug

rimmed with cobweb cracks.

*

Lord, it is hard to love
your people, so fast they go
thru drive-thrus. May I

instead love the leftover
piles of hairs in salons falling
with little scissor clicks

from their temples?
You've numbered each feathered
and bleached inch, how

in the grout they congregate.

*

Why are there beings
instead of nothings?

Martin Heidegger wondered
sometime in 1926.
Good question.

*

Lord—those wipers leaping up,
and leaping up—how to
switch them off for good?

*

On their way thru this life,
people buy a lot of things—
100% human hair, for example,

and seasonal window-clings. I live
above a convenience store
and listen to their midnight

movements, sleepless and impossible
to love shuffling, canned peaches
knocking each other

in the bottoms of their baskets.
Sometimes the *beep beep*
of the barcode-reader slips

into my dreams. Sometimes
it is the sound the Lord makes
snipping split ends off

my soul. Will it grow back, I ask
hunching in my midnight-filled
balcony—the wind flirting

my earlobes, tipping over
my recycling bin. What is it to be
thru this life? An echo.

A shorn soul? An echo.
Like windshield wipers slapping
at a storm, I miss the boy

who spoke with computers.
In the city we lived in together
he may be bringing into being

small software, a simple device
for organizing photos.

2

I am not thinking about you
It is a new way of thinking about you.
—Suzanne Buffam

Heidegger went rummaging around
being, asking, *What is it?* Threw
some language at it to see

what would happen. What happened:
being-with, being-toward,
thrownness and my favourite,

potentiality-of-being-one's-self.
Though its language sets my hair
afire, I do not understand it. My being

loiters on the furniture, variously
accumulating. Sometimes
I lift it to vacuum. I round up

my soggy recycling and set it inside
to collect another week. So we continue
separately. So, cafés/coffee shops—being

around beings without *being-with*
them, letting my mind stir-stick
someone else's ideas—the quick brown

fox—refracting my gaze
off the granite condiment stand.
For me, the difference between

café and coffee shop, Jeremy says,
is semantics and socioeconomic status.
Coffee is ubiquitous. Every hour,

the baristas dump the dregs
and brew again. Strangers pour
continuously thru, holding tenderly

their paper bags of chocolate pain.
How lovely or uniformly dressed
the baristas, Jeremy says

and his voice drips thru my being,
splashes the lazy dog of it.

*

Strangers pour language
into each other, fogging
the windows. The more they talk,

the less I'm sure what goes on
in my being and what's just human
spillage, an alphabetical blurring—

Yeah, could I get a small coffee
and a chocolate croissant? With room
for cream. I'll have that to stay.

*

The Lord led me to a city
with a dripping, concrete sky
and fourteen thousand coffee

joints. Could coffee be my authentic
being? It sure wallops me, leaves
me dry-mouthed, wildly headached

with enough aura to hear sirens
before emergencies. *Whether*
they call them pastries or baked

goods, says Jeremy. Weather
they call coastal, whipping up clouds,
to-and-froing grey gallons of seagulls.

*

The Lord said, *Get going.* Shuffling
about the desert, the people
replied, *Where to?*

*

Trying not to think
of the boy, the sound he made
when I left him, a wailing sort of

sigh. How speaking
the boy brings closer the boy.
So I don't speak

of him. So separately
we continue. So, coffee
shops/cafés—being without beings

around being with them.

*

On their breaks, Jeremy
and the jacketless Heidegger
slouch across from me.

A steady downpour of strangers.
This weather we've been
having. Someone chases an umbrella

across my window-sized sightline.
So separately we. The wind
tips over. Spilling in

all directions. Brewing again
behind tinted windows—
seeing without being seen.

3

after too much midnight, it is pleasant
to hear the milkman
—Wallace Stevens

Various doors and windows
slam thru my being, the possibles
I didn't arrive at, arriving

instead in this apartment with night
knocking about, kicking the canned
beings. I was loved under a sky

skewered by football
goalposts. I was loved in post-it notes
on the headboard, in roadside

turnouts with rain shadows
freckling my forearms.
A droning love left out

on the counter, the toward-which
of the soul. Benjamin told
the computer I was over

and it flashed its movies and games
excitedly into us. Into Moses,
the Lord poured the Fear

of the Lord, gave him ten plagues,
broke the sea into two pieces
and handed it to him—*Take this and run.*

*

Wednesday darkens. A few black
taxis drive up major roads
on quiet hazy nights. I woke in

the mourning with a fridge
full of hot dog garnishes
with cowlicked soul

and ten o'clock sadness. So
I bought hot dogs, so I wandered
into a different life

where garbage men bang
their indecipherable route
each morning across my being,

shattering my asleep,
their truck puffing out
contributions to the grey.

*

With my mouth I poured
regret and goodbye into Benjamin
and moved far away.

*

Though we live in being, Heidegger
tells me, it is the furthest thing
from our understanding,

like his ungainly tome, six inches
from my face, but it might
as well be shipped to China to be

factoried into paper trinkets.
Metaphorically many birds
thwack continuously into

my being. They do not see it. Again
my being is continuously responsible
for the death of many

metaphorical birds. Again today
darkens into the next today
and I don't know why I left him.

If I read a page a day I might
for 1.5 years manage *Being
and Time*, but then there are more

Heideggers, more ideas pinning
being into language. Could language
be my authentic being? Already

Jeremy is Hegeling with a customer
over milk-fat percentages,
Adornoing his pastry case.

*

Enough philosophy. Greatly
I have coffeed and greatly
misunderstood what people

with language communicate
into each other, what language
communicates into. I thought

the Lord was leading me
toward the dessert. Pack
my box with five-dozen

liquor jugs. The Lord said, *You*
are a dumb stubborn people I love.
And the Lord said, *I will be*

your hairdresser and you will be
my hairdo. The voice
in the wilderness. The voice

troubling up the silence,
the alphabetical burning.
The people replied, *The five*

boxing wizards jump quickly.
The Holy Spirit burned them
to the desert. The voice

careening through the soul.
Lord, the people said,
where are we going?

And Lord, Moses said, *how will we*
know once we get there? The people
watched the smoke of the Lord

barrelling the Lord's commandments
down the mountain. So the people
settled into their confusion.

They ate, slept and wandered
around their confusion, grumbling
periodically into the Lord. Morning

unrolled the long scroll
of the desert. The people tried
not to covet each other's oxen

and wives. They murdered
their neighbours less frequently.
Jeremy waxes philosophically

the floors and I understand
very little, but I hope somewhere
Benjamin is still speaking

softly into computers.
Whatever else, the Lord
keeps us walking.

Like wind-up
toys, we keep walking
and walking.

NOTES ON THE POEMS

FOR PLAY and GERTRUDE STEIN LOVES A GIRL are inspired by the work of Gertrude Stein

A FEW BOYS, JULY 1997 is based on the murders of Mike Mauro, David Nunes and Mark Teves by Kevin Vermett.

VICTORIA SOTO is the name of a teacher who was killed during the Sandy Hook school shooting.

POEM FOR JEFF is dedicated to Jeff Noh.

POETRY SHORTAGE borrows the line "Time does not finish a poem" from Jack Spicer's "Imaginary Elegies"

MANY METAPHORICAL BIRDS is for Jeremy Arnott, the most philosophical of baristas. Epigrams and quotes were taken from Heidegger's *Language* and *Being and Time*, Suzanne Buffam's "Vanishing Interior," and a Wallace Stevens letter from 1928. Many common pangrams, as well as quotes and narrative elements from the Book of Exodus, have also been appropriated throughout the poem.

ACKNOWLEDGEMENTS

Poems from this book have appeared previously in *This Side of West*, *ARC Poetry Magazine*, *The Malahat Review*, *qwerty*, *CV2*, *The Antigonish Review*, *Best Canadian Poetry in English 2012*, *The New Quarterly*, *The Walrus*, *The Maynard*, *The Literary Review of Canada*, *The Quilliad* and *The Fiddlehead*. Thank you to the editors of each.

Thank you to my parents, Brenda and John Czaga, for their support and understanding.

Thank you to Zaq, the best first reader.

Thank you to the teachers, peers and friends who have helped me throughout the process of writing and editing this book, especially Rhea Tregebov, advisor extraordinaire.

Thank you to everyone at Nightwood for making this book a reality—Silas White for his careful editing, Heather Lohnes for her encouragement, and Carleton Wilson for the book's gorgeous cover and design.

ABOUT THE AUTHOR

Kayla Czaga grew up in Kitimat, BC, and currently lives in Vancouver, where she recently earned her MFA in Creative Writing at UBC. She won *The Malahat Review*'s 2012 Far Horizons Award for Poetry and *The Fiddlehead*'s 23rd Annual Ralph Gustafson Poetry Prize. *For Your Safety Please Hold On* is her first book.